The Big Dog

Written by Roger Carr
Illustrated by Maggie Dannatt

TM
sundance
A Haights Cross Communications Company

"Spike! Come back!" Jane cried.
But it was too late.

Spike had crawled under the fence.
He ran into the spooky old garden
of the empty house next door.

3

Jane looked over the fence.
"Spike!" she called. "Spike! Spike!"

But Spike did not come.

So Jane climbed over the fence
and into the spooky garden.

Suddenly a big dog appeared
and started chasing Spike.

Where had the big dog come from?
Jane had never seen it before.

At the end of the path,
there was an old shed.
Spike ran into the shed.
Jane ran in after him and slammed
the door shut. They were safe.

8

Jane could hear the big dog barking.
"Go away!" Jane shouted. "Go away!"

She finally heard the dog leave.

"Let's go, Spike," she said,
and pulled on the door to open it.

But the door would not open. It was stuck.

"Help!" Jane cried. "Please help me!"
No one could hear her.

Jane looked for a way out of the shed.
She saw a small hole in one wall.

It was too small for her,
but it was big enough for Spike.

12

Jane found some paper and a pencil. "Mom, help me," she wrote. "I'm stuck in the old shed next door."

She tied the note to Spike's collar, and pushed him through the hole.

"Home, Spike!" she said. "Go home!"

The big dog chased Spike
through the garden.
Spike ran under the fence.
He was home.

He barked and barked until Jane's mother came out of the house.

She read the note on his collar.
"Come on, Spike," she said.
"Let's get Jane."

"Oh, Mom," Jane cried. "I was so worried. I thought that big dog would hurt Spike!"

"A new family is moving into
the house next door," said Jane's mom.

"The big dog belongs to them.
I think he was just saying hello.
He wants to be friends with Spike!"